Contents

The Managers

1) Name every permanent manager of Newcastle United in the 21st Century from the years given
1999-2004
2004-2006
2006-2007
2007-2008
2008
2008-2009
2009
2009-2010
2010-2014
2015
2015-2016
2016-2019
2019-

The 21st Century

1) Which Aston Villa player scored a last-minute equaliser against Brighton in the final game of the 2016/17 Championship season to secure the title for Newcastle?

2) Leon best scored a hat trick against which side in 2011?

3) Who made his debut for the club after coming on for the injured Rob Elliot in a 2-1 victory over Chelsea in 2014?

4) Who scored Newcastle's last ever goal at Maine Road in a 1-0 win?

5) Who took over as captain of Newcastle in 2006 after Alan Shearer retired?

6) Just weeks after signing for the club, Hatem Ben Arfa had his leg broken in a challenge from which Manchester City player?

7) Who scored Newcastle's 1000th Premier League goal?

8) Steve Harper long service ended after he left the club to join who permanently?

9) Which player had a spectacular long-range goal controversially ruled out for offside against Manchester City in 2014?

10) Manager Alan Pardew was given a ban after headbutting which Hull City player?

11) Who crucially had a goal ruled out against Fulham in May of 2009 as Newcastle slid closer to relegation?

12) Who scored an own goal at Villa Park as Newcastle were relegated in 2009?

Transfers

1) Andy Carroll left to join which club in January 2011?

2) Which two long-serving players left to join Derby County in 2002?

3) Nikos Dabizas left Newcastle to join which side?

4) Michael Owen joined for a club record fee from Real Madrid in what year?

5) Which defender returned to the club for a second spell in 2006 but failed to make any appearances before being released?

6) Which legendary former goalkeeper returned for a brief spell in 2006?

7) Shola Ameobi made a loan move to which side in 2008?

8) After the club's relegation, Sebastien Bassong move to which club?

9) Yohan Cabaye was signed from which French club?

10) Ayoze Perez arrived from where in 2014?

11) Which player crossed the Tyne-Wear divide by signing from Sunderland in 2014?

12) Which two players did Newcastle sign from Nottingham Forest in 2014?

First Goals

Can you name the teams these players scored against to register their first goal for Newcastle?

1) Papiss Cisse
a. Swansea
b. Aston Villa
c. Chelsea

2) Andy Carroll
a. West Ham
b. Stoke
c. Manchester City

3) David Edgar
a. Liverpool
b. Manchester United
c. Arsenal

4) Paul Dummett
a. Liverpool
b. Manchester United
c. Southampton

5) Joelinton
a. West Ham
b. Everton
c. Tottenham

6) Demba Ba
a. Tottenham
b. Reading
c. Blackburn Rovers

7) Yohan Cabaye
a. Manchester United
b. West Ham
c. Wigan

8) Patrick Kluivert
a. Aston Villa
b. Middlesbrough
c. Everton

9) Laurent Robert
a. Middlesbrough
b. Everton
c. Birmingham City

10) Loic Remy
a. Hull
b. QPR
c. Cardiff

11) Craig Bellamy
a. Lokeren
b. Partizan Belgrade
c. Royal Antwerp

Red Cards

1)   Who was sent off as Newcastle drew 1-1 with Sunderland in October 2012?

2)   Which Newcastle player was sent off during the 3-0 Tyne-Wear derby loss in October 2015, only to have his suspension overturned on appeal?

3)   Who was controversially sent off as Newcastle drew 2-2 with Manchester City in 2008?

4)   Who received his first career red card in the home match with Manchester United in 2019?

5)   Which centre back was dismissed during a Premier League game with Liverpool in March 2006?

6) Who was sent off in a 2002 Champions League Second Group Stage match for kicking out at Marco Materazzi in the opening stages of a loss to Inter Milan?

7) Which two players were sent off in an away match against Liverpool in 2014?

8) Which two players were sent off as Newcastle slipped to a 3-0 defeat away at Leicester in 2015?

9) Newcastle had Jonjo Shelvey and Paul Dummett dismissed in a controversial encounter against Nottingham Forest in 2016. What was the name of the referee who sent off the pair?

10) Who was sent off against Manchester City in the first game of the 2013 season?

11) Jonjo Shelvey was sent off in the first game of the 2017/18 season after stamping on which spurs player?

12) Jamall Lascelles was sent off in 2016 during a 3-0 away loss to which side?

13) Against Aston Villa in 2005 Newcastle were reduced to eight men after which three players were dismissed?

The 21st Century II

1) Which team did Newcastle defeat to give Alan Shearer his only win as Newcastle manager?

2) Which former Newcastle player ended up playing in goal for Liverpool at St James' Park after Pepe Reina was sent off in 2012?

3) Who was given a red card after attempting to punch Alan Shearer in the meeting between Newcastle and Manchester United in 2001?

4) In what year did Mike Ashley complete his takeover of the club?

5) Who took the number 9 shirt after Alan Shearer retired in 2006?

6) In which two years did Newcastle win the Championship?

7) Who did Newcastle beat 2-0 on the last day of the 2014/15 season to ensure their survival?

8) Alan Shearer was manager for how many games?

9) Obafemi Martins scored two penalties in the Premier League for Newcastle, what was unusual about them?

10) What has been Newcastle's highest league finish this century?

Transfers II

1) Gini Wijnaldum was signed in 2015 from which Dutch team?

2) From which club was Aleksandar Mitrovic signed in 2015?

3) Steve Taylor joined which MLS side after leaving Newcastle?

4) Which Spanish midfielder signed from Borussia Dortmund in 2017?

5) Which centre back was signed from Deportivo in 2018?

6) Miguel Almiron arrived in January 2019 from which American team?

7) Newcastle broke their transfer record to sign Joelinton in 2019 from which German side?

8) Carl Cort joined in the year 2000 from which club?

9) Which strike did Newcastle sign from Coventry in 2001?

10) Laurent Robert was signed from which French club in 2001?

11) Who signed on a free from Barcelona in 2004?

12) Jonathan Woodgate left for which side in 2004?

13) Which midfielder re-signed for Newcastle from Fulham in 2005?

Memorable Goals

1) Ryan Taylor scored his famous free kick against Sunderland in 2011, but who was in goal for the opposition?

2) Ryan Taylor scored a brilliant dipping volley at the Gallowgate end against which opposition in 2011?

3) Charles N'zogbia scored a long range effort with his right foot in a 2-2 draw against who in 2007?

4) Matty Longstaff scored an unforgettable debut goal against which side in a 1-0 win?

5) Alan Shearer scored his final ever goal by scoring a penalty in the Tyne-Wear derby past which goalkeeper?

6) Papiss Cisse won the goal of the season award for his stunning effort against Chelsea in which year?

7) Laurent Robert scored a magnificent brace in a 4-0 win against who in 2003?

8) Obafemi Martins scored a screamer as Newcastle beat Spurs by what scoreline in 2007?

9) Which player scored his only goal for Newcastle in the same match?

10) Alan Shearer struck a ferocious volley against Everton in December 2002, but which goalkeeper did he beat with the strike?

11) Fabian Schar won the Premier League goal of the month for his strike against who in February 2019?

12) Alan Shearer became the club's leading goal scorer of all time when he scored against which team?

Memorable Games

1) In the remarkable 4-4 draw with Arsenal in 2011 which Arsenal player was sent off?

2) Newcastle hammered Sunderland 5-1 in 2010, but who scored the Sunderland consolation goal?

3) Who scored a hat trick as Newcastle beat Aston Villa 6-0 in 2010?

4) Who scored an own goal at Villa Park on the last day of the 2008/09 season as Newcastle were relegated to the Championship?

5) Newcastle sealed the Championship title in 2010 with a 2-0 away win against Plymouth, who scored the second goal?

6) Who scored two goals on his home debut as Chelsea were beaten 3-2 at St James' Park in 2013?

7) Newcastle went top of the Premier League table for Christmas 2001 by winning 3-1 away against which team?

8) Newcastle won 4-3 in Bobby Robson's 100th match in charge against which side in 2001?

9) Newcastle lost a pre-season friendly 6-1 to which lower league side in 2009?

10) Newcastle conceded 11 goals in two games in December 2012 with a 4-3 then 7-3 loss against which teams?

11) Who was sent off as Newcastle were embarrassed by a 6-0 loss to Liverpool in 2013?

12) Who scored the consolation as Liverpool hammered Newcastle 5-1 in 2008?

13) Who won the man of the match award as Newcastle won 1-0 away at Tottenham in 2013?

14) Who scored the only goal at Old Trafford in 2013 as Newcastle secured their first away win against Manchester United since 1972?

15) Which player scored four goals at Newcastle trounced Norwich 6-2 in 2015?

16) Who scored the first goal as Newcastle beat Manchester United 3-0 in February 2000?

17) Who scored an own goal for Manchester United as they lost 3-0 to Newcastle at St James' Park in 2012?

First Goals II

1) Habib Beye
a. Birmingham City
b. Wigan
c. Fulham

2) Obafemi Martins
a. Tottenham
b. Reading
c. West Ham

3) Kevin Nolan
a. Everton
b. Crystal Palace
c. Bolton

4) Jonas Gutierrez
a. Doncaster
b. Peterborough United
c. Bristol City

5) Hatem Ben Arfa
a. Bolton
b. Everton
c. Blackburn

6) Gael Bigirimana
a. Bolton
b. Wigan
c. Blackburn

7) Haris Vuckic
a. Maritimo
b. Atromitos
c. Club Brugge

8) Sylvain Marveaux
a. Maritimo
b. Atromitos
c. Club Brugge

9) Fabrice Pancrate
a. West Brom
b. West Ham
c. Watford

10) Carl Cort
a. Leicester City
b. Derby County
c. Coventry City

Cup games

1) In the FA Cup semi-final loss against Chelsea in the year 2000, which player scored twice against Newcastle as they went down to a 2-1 defeat?

2) Newcastle were knocked out of the FA Cup at the 3rd round stage in 2011 after losing 3-1 to which lower league side?

3) Which side defeated Newcastle as they slumped to a 3-0 defeat away from home in the 2017 FA Cup 4th round?

4) Birmingham knocked Newcastle out of the 2007 FA Cup in a replay at St James' Park, but what was the score?

5) Sammy and Shola Ameobi made history by scoring a goal each as Newcastle beat which side in the League Cup in 2013?

6) Hull defeated Newcastle on penalties in 2017 at the quarter final stage of the League Cup, who missed penalties for the magpies?

7) Who scored a last minute winner as Chelsea knocked Newcastle out of the League Cup in 2001?

8) Newcastle suffered an embarrassing FA Cup Semi-Final loss in 2005 to Manchester United, what was the score?

9) Which team knocked Newcastle out the League Cup at the 3rd round stage in 2009?

10) Who did Newcastle lose to in both 2012 and 2013 to be eliminated from the FA Cup?

11) Newcastle caused an upset by knocking Manchester City out of the league cup in 2014, but who scored the opening goal in the 2-0 win?

12) Newcastle lost to which Premier League side on penalties to be knocked out of the 2019/20 League Cup?

13) Who scored his only ever Newcastle goal against Blackburn Rovers in the FA Cup in 2019, before being released that summer?

Transfers III

1)   From which Spanish side did Newcastle purchase Albert Luque in 2005?

2)   Who re-joined the club from Aston Villa in 2005?

3)   Which Manchester United player did Newcastle sign on a six month loan deal in 2006?

4)   Which former Manchester City player did Newcastle sign on a free in the closing hours of the 2006 summer transfer window?

5)   Michael Chopra signed for which club when he left Newcastle in 2006?

6)   Jean-Alain Boumsong left Newcastle to join which Italian club in 2006?

7)   Jonas Gutierrez signed from where in 2008?

8)   Future captain Fabricio Coloccini was signed from which Spanish club in 2008?

9)   Peter Løvenkrands was signed on a free from which German club in January 2009?

10) For which club did James Milner leave to join in 2008?

11) Shay Given left to join Manchester City on February the 1st of which year?

12) Goalkeeper Rob Elliot was signed from where in 2011?

13) Which club did Newcastle sign Papiss Cisse from in 2012?

14) Mapou Yanga-Mbiwa was sold to which Italian club in 2014?

15) Who did Newcastle sign in January 2016 from Tottenham to help in their fight against relegation?

16) Who did Davide Santon join when he left Newcastle in 2015?

European games

1) Who scored the winner as Newcastle sealed a dramatic 3-2 away win in the Champions League against Feyenoord in 2002?

2) The win against Feyenoord made Champions League history as Newcastle became the first side to achieve what?

3) Who scored the only goal as Newcastle beat Juventus in the 2002/03 Champions League?

4) Which two players made their debuts in a memorable away match against Palermo in 2006?

5) Newcastle went out of the Champions League at the qualifying round in 2003, losing on penalties to which team?

6) Alan Shearer scored a Champions League hat trick against which German side in 2003?

7) In 2004 Newcastle lost the Semi-Final of the Uefa Cup 2-0 on aggregate to Marseille. Which future Premier League striker scored both goals in the second leg?

8) Papiss Cisse scored in the last minute of the second-leg to give Newcastle a 1-0 aggregate victory in a Europa League match against who in 2013?

9) Newcastle lost 2-0 at home to Barcelona in a 2003 Champions League game, which future Magpie scored for the opposition?

10) Which Norwegian side did Newcastle knock out of the UEFA Cup in 2004?

11) Newcastle drew both group stage games against which Portuguese team in the 2012/13 Europa League?

Answers

The Managers

1) Name every permanent manager of Newcastle United in the 21st Century from the years given

Bobby Robson 1999-2004
Graeme Souness 2004-2006
Glenn Roeder 2006-2007
Sam Allardyce 2007-2008
Kevin Keegan 2008
Joe Kinnear 2008-2009
Alan Shearer 2009
Chris Hughton 2009-2010
Alan Pardew 2010-2014
John Carver 2015
Steve McClaren 2015-2016
Rafael Benitez 2016-2019
Steve Bruce 2019

The 21st Century

1)   Which Aston Villa player scored a last-minute equaliser against Brighton in the final game of the 2016/17 Championship season to secure the title for Newcastle?
Jack Grealish

2)   Leon best scored a hat trick against which side in 2011?
West Ham

3)   Who made his debut for the club after coming on for the injured Rob Elliot in a 2-1 victory over Chelsea in 2014?
Jak Alnwick

4)   Who scored Newcastle's last ever goal at Maine Road in a 1-0 win?
Alan Shearer

5)   Who took over as captain of Newcastle in 2006 after Alan Shearer retired?
Scott Parker

6) Just weeks after signing for the club, Hatem Ben Arfa had his leg broken in a challenge from which Manchester City player?
Nigel de Jong

7) Who scored Newcastle's 1000th Premier League goal?
Demba Ba

8) Steve Harper long service ended after he left the club to join who permanently?
Hull City

9) Which player had a spectacular long-range goal controversially ruled out for offside against Manchester City in 2014?
Cheick Tiote

10) Manager Alan Pardew was given a ban after headbutting which Hull City player?
David Meyler

11) Who crucially had a goal ruled out against Fulham in May of 2009 as Newcastle slid closer to relegation?
Mark Viduka

12) Who scored an own goal at Villa Park as Newcastle were relegated in 2009?
Damien Duff

Transfers

1)   Andy Carroll left to join which club in January 2011?
Liverpool

2)   Which two long-serving players left to join Derby County in 2002?
Rob Lee and Warren Barton

3)   Nikos Dabizas left Newcastle to join which side?
Leicester City

4)   Michael Owen joined for a club record fee from Real Madrid in what year?
2005

5)   Which defender returned to the club for a second spell in 2006 but failed to make any appearances before being released?
Olivier Bernard

6) Which legendary former goalkeeper returned for a brief spell in 2006?
Pavel Srnicek

7) Shola Ameobi made a loan move to which side in 2008?
Stoke City

8) After the club's relegation, Sebastien Bassong move to which club?
Tottenham

9) Yohan Cabaye was signed from which French club?
Lille

10) Ayoze Perez arrived from where in 2014?
Tenerife

11) Which player crossed the Tyne-Wear divide by signing from Sunderland in 2014?
Jack Colback

12) Which two players did Newcastle sign from Nottingham Forest in 2014?
Jamaal Lascelles and Karl Darlow

First Goals

1) Papiss Cisse
Aston Villa

2) Andy Carroll
West Ham

3) David Edgar
Manchester United

4) Paul Dummett
Liverpool

5) Joelinton
Tottenham

6) Demba Ba
Blackburn Rovers

7) Yohan Cabaye
Wigan

8) Patrick Kluivert
Aston Villa

9) Laurent Robert
Middlesbrough

10) Loic Remy
Hull

11) Craig Bellamy
Lokeren

Red Cards

1) Who was sent off as Newcastle drew 1-1 with Sunderland in October 2012?
Cheick Tiote

2) Which Newcastle player was sent off during the 3-0 Tyne-Wear derby loss in October 2015, only to have his suspension overturned on appeal?
Fabricio Coloccini

3) Who was controversially sent off as Newcastle drew 2-2 with Manchester City in 2008?
Habib Beye

4) Who received his first career red card in the home match with Manchester United in 2019?
Sean Longstaff

5) Which centre back was dismissed during a Premier League game with Liverpool in March 2006?
Jean-Alain Boumsong

6)   Who was sent off in a 2002 Champions League Second Group Stage match for kicking out at Marco Materazzi in the opening stages of a loss to Inter Milan?
Craig Bellamy

7)   Which two players were sent off in an away match against Liverpool in 2014?
Paul Dummett and Shola Ameobi

8)   Which two players were sent off as Newcastle slipped to a 3-0 defeat away at Leicester in 2015?
Mike Williamson and Daryl Janmaat

9)   Newcastle had Jonjo Shelvey and Paul Dummett dismissed in a controversial encounter against Nottingham Forest in 2016. What was the name of the referee who sent off the pair?
Steve Martin

10) Who was sent off against Manchester City in the first game of the 2013 season?

Steven Taylor

11) Jonjo Shelvey was sent off in the first game of the 2017/18 season after stamping on which spurs player?

Dele Alli

12) Jamall Lascelles was sent off in 2016 during a 3-0 away loss to which side?

Everton

13) Against Aston Villa in 2005 Newcastle were reduced to eight men after which three players were dismissed?

Lee Bowyer, Kieron Dyer and Steven Taylor

The 21st Century II

1) Which team did Newcastle defeat to give Alan Shearer his only win as Newcastle manager?
Middlesbrough

2) Which former Newcastle player ended up playing in goal for Liverpool at St James' Park after Pepe Reina was sent off in 2012?
Jose Enrique

3) Who was given a red card after attempting to punch Alan Shearer in the meeting between Newcastle and Manchester United in 2001?
Roy Keane

4) In what year did Mike Ashley complete his takeover of the club?
2007

5) Who took the number 9 shirt after Alan Shearer retired in 2006?
Obafemi Martins

6) In which two years did Newcastle win the Championship?
2010 and 2017

7) Who did Newcastle beat 2-0 on the last day of the 2014/15 season to ensure their survival?
West Ham

8) Alan Shearer was manager for how many games?
Eight

9) Obafemi Martins scored two penalties in the Premier League for Newcastle, what was unusual about them?
One was with his right foot, one with his left

10) What has been Newcastle's highest league finish this century?
3rd in the 2002/03 season

Transfers II

1) Gini Wijnaldum was signed in 2015 from which Dutch team?
PSV Eindhoven

2) From which club was Aleksandar Mitrovic signed in 2015?
Anderlecht

3) Steve Taylor joined which MLS side after leaving Newcastle?
Portland Timbers

4) Which Spanish midfielder signed from Borussia Dortmund in 2017?
Mikel Merino

5) Which centre back was signed from Deportivo in 2018?
Fabian Schar

6) Miguel Almiron arrived in January 2019 from which American team?
Atlanta

7)   Newcastle broke their transfer record to sign Joelinton in 2019 from which German side?
Hoffenheim

8)   Carl Cort joined in the year 2000 from which club?
Wimbledon

9)   Which strike did Newcastle sign from Coventry in 2001?
Craig Bellamy

10) Laurent Robert was signed from which French club in 2001?
Paris Saint-Germain

11) Who signed on a free from Barcelona in 2004?
Patrick Kluivert

12) Jonathan Woodgate left for which side in 2004?
Real Madrid

13) Which midfielder re-signed for Newcastle from Fulham in 2005?
Lee Clark

Memorable Goals

1) Ryan Taylor scored his famous free kick against Sunderland in 2011, but who was in goal for the opposition?
Simon Mignolet

2) Ryan Taylor scored a brilliant dipping volley at the Gallowgate end against which opposition in 2011?
Everton

3) Charles N'zogbia scored a long range effort with his right foot in a 2-2 draw against who in 2007?
Middlesbrough

4) Matty Longstaff scored an unforgettable debut goal against which side in a 1-0 win?
Manchester United

5) Alan Shearer scored his final ever goal by scoring a penalty in the Tyne-Wear derby past which goalkeeper?
Kelvin Davis

6) Papiss Cisse won the goal of the season award for his stunning effort against Chelsea in which year?
2012

7) Laurent Robert scored a magnificent brace in a 4-0 win against who in 2003?
Tottenham

8) Obafemi Martins scored a screamer as Newcastle beat Spurs by what scoreline in 2007?
3-2

9) Which player scored his only goal for Newcastle in the same match?
Paul Huntington

10) Alan Shearer struck a ferocious volley against Everton in December 2002, but which goalkeeper did he beat with the strike?
Richard Wright

11) Fabian Schar won the Premier League goal of the month for his strike against who in February 2019?
Burnley

12) Alan Shearer became the club's leading goal scorer of all time when he scored against which team?
Portsmouth

Memorable Games

1) In the remarkable 4-4 draw with
Arsenal in 2011 which Arsenal player was
sent off?
Abou Diaby

2) Newcastle hammered Sunderland 5-
1 in 2010, but who scored the
Sunderland consolation goal?
Darren Bent

3) Who scored a hat trick as Newcastle
beat Aston Villa 6-0 in 2010?
Andy Carroll

4) Who scored an own goal at Villa Park
on the last day of the 2008/09 season as
Newcastle were relegated to the
Championship?
Damien Duff

5) Newcastle sealed the Championship
title in 2010 with a 2-0 away win against
Plymouth, who scored the second goal?
Wayne Routledge

6) Who scored two goals on his home debut as Chelsea were beaten 3-2 at St James' Park in 2013?
Moussa Sissoko

7) Newcastle went top of the Premier League table for Christmas 2001 by winning 3-1 away against which team?
Arsenal

8) Newcastle won 4-3 in Bobby Robson's 100th match in charge against which side in 2001?
Manchester United

9) Newcastle lost a pre-season friendly 6-1 to which lower league side in 2009?
Leyton Orient

10) Newcastle conceded 11 goals in two games in December 2012 with a 4-3 then 7-3 loss against which teams?
Manchester United and Arsenal

11) Who was sent off as Newcastle were embarrassed by a 6-0 loss to Liverpool in 2013?
Mathieu Debuchy

12) Who scored the consolation as Liverpool hammered Newcastle 5-1 in 2008?
David Edgar

13) Who won the man of the match award as Newcastle won 1-0 away at Tottenham in 2013?
Tim Krul

14) Who scored the only goal at Old Trafford in 2013 as Newcastle secured their first away win against Manchester United since 1972?
Yohan Cabaye

15) Which player scored four goals at Newcastle trounced Norwich 6-2 in 2015?
Georginio Wijnaldum

16) Who scored the first goal as Newcastle beat Manchester United 3-0 in February 2000?
Duncan Ferguson

17) Who scored an own goal for Manchester United as they lost 3-0 to Newcastle at St James' Park in 2012?
Phil Jones

First Goals II

1) Habib Beye
Birmingham City

2) Obafemi Martins
West Ham

3) Kevin Nolan
Crystal Palace

4) Jonas Gutierrez
Peterborough United

5) Hatem Ben Arfa
Everton

6) Gael Bigirimana
Wigan

7) Haris Vuckic
Atromitos

8) Sylvain Marveaux
Maritimo

9) Fabrice Pancrate
Watford

10) Carl Cort
Derby County

Cup Games

1) In the FA Cup semi-final loss against Chelsea in the year 2000, which player scored twice against Newcastle as they went down to a 2-1 defeat?
Gus Poyet

2) Newcastle were knocked out of the FA Cup at the 3rd round stage in 2011 after losing 3-1 to which lower league side?
Stevenage Borough

3) Which side defeated Newcastle as they slumped to a 3-0 defeat away from home in the 2017 FA Cup 4th round?
Oxford United

4) Birmingham knocked Newcastle out of the 2007 FA Cup in a replay at St James' Park, but what was the score?
5-1

5) Sammy and Shola Ameobi made history by scoring a goal each as Newcastle beat which side in the League Cup in 2013?
Morecambe

6) Hull defeated Newcastle on penalties in 2017 at the quarter final stage of the League Cup, who missed penalties for the magpies?
Jonjo Shelvey, Dwight Gayle and Yoan Gouffran

7) Who scored a last-minute winner as Chelsea knocked Newcastle out of the League Cup in 2001?
Jimmy Floyd Hasselbaink

8) Newcastle suffered an embarrassing FA Cup Semi-Final loss in 2005 to Manchester United, what was the score?
4-1

9) Which team knocked Newcastle out the League Cup at the 3rd round stage in 2009?
Peterborough

10) Who did Newcastle lose to in both 2012 and 2013 to be eliminated from the FA Cup?
Brighton

11) Newcastle caused an upset by knocking Manchester City out of the league cup in 2014, but who scored the opening goal in the 2-0 win?
Rolando Aarons

12) Newcastle lost to which Premier League side on penalties to be knocked out of the 2019/20 League Cup?
Leicester City

13) Who scored his only ever Newcastle goal against Blackburn Rovers in the FA Cup in 2019, before being released that summer?
Callum Roberts

Transfers III

1)   From which Spanish side did Newcastle purchase Albert Luque in 2005?
Deportivo de La Coruna

2)   Who re-joined the club from Aston Villa in 2005?
Nolberto Solano

3)   Which Manchester United player did Newcastle sign on a six month loan deal in 2006?
Guiseppe Rossi

4)   Which former Manchester City player did Newcastle sign on a free in the closing hours of the 2006 summer transfer window?
Antoine Sibierski

5)   Michael Chopra signed for which club when he left Newcastle in 2006?
Cardiff

6) Jean-Alain Boumsong left Newcastle to join which Italian club in 2006?
Juventus

7) Jonas Gutierrez signed from where in 2008?
Mallorca

8) Future captain Fabricio Coloccini was signed from which Spanish club in 2008?
Deportivo de La Coruna

9) Peter Løvenkrands was signed on a free from which German club in January 2009?
Schalke

10) For which club did James Milner leave to join in 2008?
Aston Villa

11) Shay Given left to join Manchester City on February the 1st of which year?
2009

12) Goalkeeper Rob Elliot was signed from where in 2011?
Charlton Athletic

13) Which club did Newcastle sign Papiss Cisse from in 2012?
Freiburg

14) Mapou Yanga-Mbiwa was sold to which Italian club in 2014?
Roma

15) Who did Newcastle sign in January 2016 from Tottenham to help in their fight against relegation?
Andros Townsend

16) Who did Davide Santon join when he left Newcastle in 2015?
Inter Milan

European Games

1)   Who scored the winner as Newcastle sealed a dramatic 3-2 away win in the Champions League against Feyenoord in 2002?
Craig Bellamy

2)   The win against Feyenoord made Champions League history as Newcastle became the first side to achieve what?
Qualifying from the group stage despite losing their first three games

3)   Who scored the only goal as Newcastle beat Juventus in the 2002/03 Champions League?
Andy Griffin

4)   Which two players made their debuts in a memorable away match against Palermo in 2006?
Tim Krul and Andy Carroll

5) Newcastle went out of the Champions League at the qualifying round in 2003, losing on penalties to which team?

Partizan Belgrade

6) Alan Shearer scored a Champions League hat trick against which German side in 2003?

Bayer Leverkusen

7) In 2004 Newcastle lost the Semi-Final of the Uefa Cup 2-0 on aggregate to Marseille. Which future Premier League striker scored both goals in the second leg?

Didier Drogba

8) Papiss Cisse scored in the last minute of the second-leg to give Newcastle a 1-0 aggregate victory in a Europa League match against who in 2013?

Anzhi Makhachkala

9) Newcastle lost 2-0 at home to Barcelona in a 2003 Champions League game, which future Magpie scored for the opposition?
Patrick Kluivert

10) Which Norwegian side did Newcastle knock out of the UEFA Cup in 2004?
Valarenga

11) Newcastle drew both group stage games against which Portuguese team in the 2012/13 Europa League?
Maritimo

Printed in Great Britain
by Amazon

47367324R00038